Copyright © 2020 Clavis Publishing Inc., New York

Originally published as *Wondere wereld. Grootse gebouwen* in Belgium and the Netherlands by Clavis Uitgeverij, 2017
English translation from the Dutch by Clavis Publishing Inc., New York

Visit us on the Web at www.clavis-publishing.com.

Mack's World of Wonder: Great Buildings written and illustrated by Mack van Gageldonk

ISBN 978-1-60537-499-4

This book was printed in April 2022 at Nikara, M. R. Štefánika 858/25, 963 01 Krupina, Slovakia.

First Edition
10 9 8 7 6 5 4

Clavis Publishing supports the First Amendment and celebrates the right to read.

GREAT BUILDINGS

Mack

Clavis

NEW YORK

INDEX

8 **BUILDINGS THEN AND NOW**
10 The First Buildings
12 Today's Buildings

14 **FAMOUS BUILDINGS**
16 The Parthenon
18 The Pantheon
20 The Colosseum
22 Petra
24 The Gravensteen
26 Himeji Castle
28 The Taj Mahal
30 The Tower of Pisa
32 Saint Basil's Cathedral
34 Neuschwanstein Castle
36 The Blue Mosque
38 The Royal Palace
   of Bangkok
40 The Palace of Versailles

42 La Sagrada Familia
44 The Big Mosque of Djenné
46 Notre-Dame Cathedral
48 Big Ben
50 The United States Capitol
52 Galeries Lafayette
54 The Sydney Opera House
56 The Empire State Building
58 Niterói Contemporary
   Art Museum (MAC)
60 The Burj Khalifa

62 **OTHER FAMOUS STRUCTURES**
64 Angkor Wat
66 The Pyramids
68 The Great Wall of China
70 Machu Picchu
72 The Eiffel Tower
74 The Golden Gate Bridge
76 The Statue of Liberty

Buildings Then and Now

THE FIRST BUILDINGS

A long, long time ago, there were no buildings yet. But people wanted to be comfortable, warm, and sheltered from the wind, rain, and snow. So they start living in caves. Later, they added doors to the caves and they carved windows in the walls. That's how the first buildings were created.

Thousands of years ago, houses were very simple.
They might have been dug into the earth with walls made of stones.
A wood fire was used to cook food and for warmth.

In which house did people live thousands of years ago?

TODAY'S BUILDINGS

High buildings in Moscow.

Now there are buildings in all shapes and sizes.
Some buildings are low and made of stone, and others are very high
and made of metal, glass, or both. Buildings also have different shapes.
Angled, crooked, round, or curved, some are really interesting.
Buildings are not only great to live or work in, but also fun to look at!

Tall cranes help to build skyscrapers.

A construction site in Dubai.

In the past, buildings were often made of brick, cement, wood, or concrete. Now other materials are used as well. The Reichstag in Berlin has a beautiful glass dome. That way everyone can look outside. And inside!

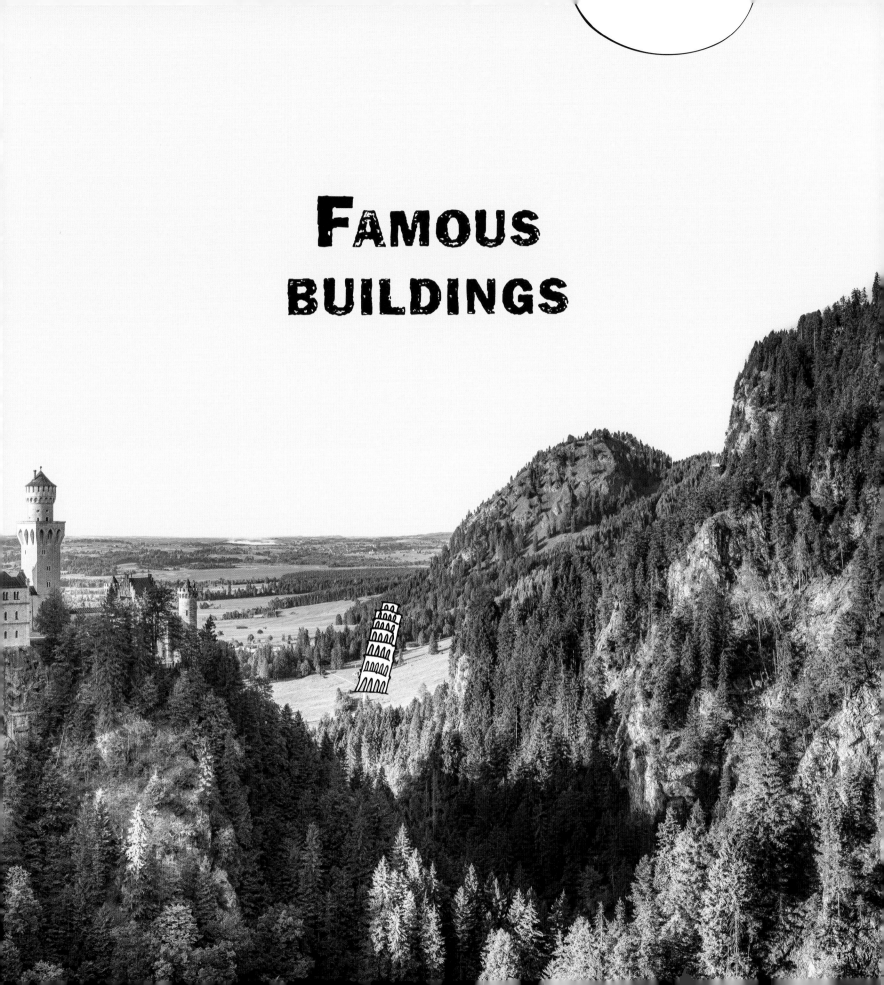

FAMOUS BUILDINGS

THE PARTHENON

Two thousand and five hundred years ago, the Greeks built a temple high on a hill in Athens: the Parthenon. Centuries later, only part of the building is still standing. This beautiful building, with its tall columns, has been used as an example for other buildings all over the world.

The columns on the Erechtheion, another temple near the Parthenon, look like women.

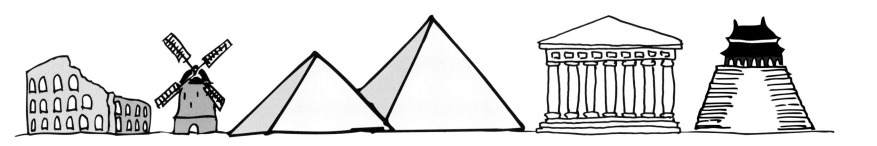

Which building looks like the Parthenon?

THE PANTHEON

The Pantheon, in the Italian capital, Rome, was built more than two thousand years ago. A hole in the center of the dome allows the sun to shine through. But it also allows rain to fall through—and birds to fly in!

The ancient Romans used the Pantheon
as a temple to worship their many gods.

How do you think these pigeons might enter the Pantheon?

THE COLOSSEUM

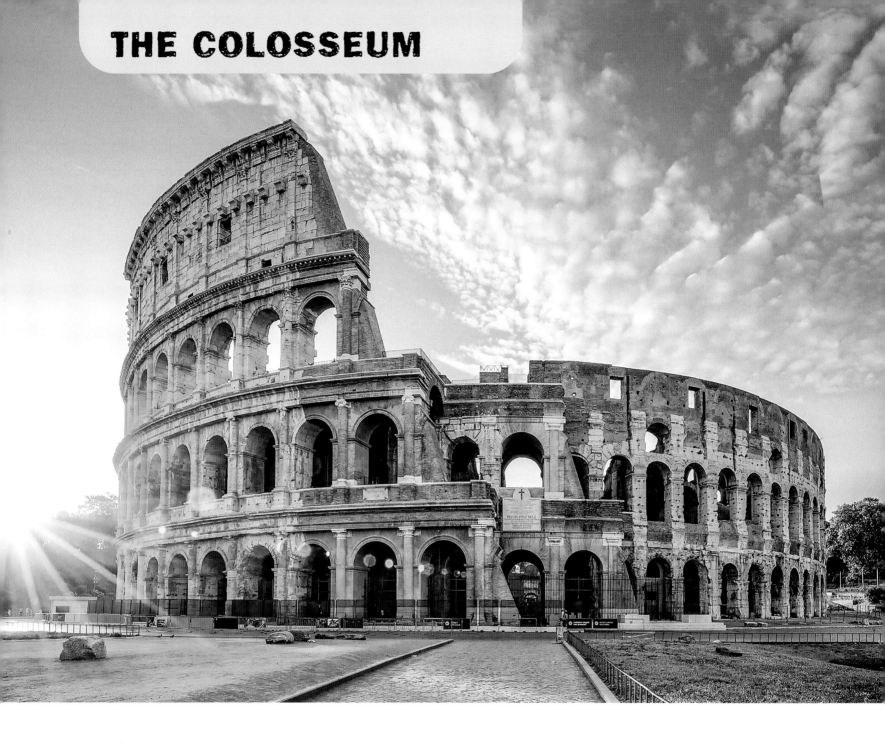

The Colosseum was also built by the Romans, two thousand years ago. It was built to be a sports arena. There was no football or hockey at that time, but people of the Roman Empire watched humans fight against each other or against wild animals such as lions, tigers, elephants, and bears.

The Colosseum was so big that as many as fifty thousand people could view the competitions at one time!

Gladiators fought in the Colosseum. Can you point to the gladiator?

PETRA

Petra is an ancient city in the middle of the desert in Jordan. The houses of Petra were not just built on the ground—they are built right into the sandstone rocks! The buildings of Petra have not been lived in for centuries, and most of them are run down. But once this city was very wealthy.

The buildings in Petra
were chopped out of rocks
with hand tools.

Which color looks like the buildings of Petra?

THE GRAVENSTEEN

In the Middle Ages, strong fortresses were built to protect cities against enemies. A moat and a thick wall around the castle provided extra protection. The Gravensteen in Ghent, Belgium, was a very strong castle built to protect the whole city. The walls are almost five feet thick. They were so thick that even cannonballs couldn't break through. Knights fired spears and arrows at their enemies from the high towers.

The Gravensteen in Ghent has many watchtowers.

How many towers does this castle have?

HIMEJI CASTLE

Himeji Castle is one of the oldest and most beautiful castles in Japan. From a boat, you can see the castle in the distance. It looks like a graceful palace, in a garden full of blossoming trees. But it really is surrounded by high and thick castle walls. Many castles in Japan have been destroyed over the years by volcanos, earthquakes, fires, and other disasters, but Himeji Castle is still standing strong.

This castle was protected by thick walls.

Himeji Castle is also called the Castle of the White Heron. Does it look like a white bird to you?

The Taj Mahal in India is one of the most beautiful buildings in the world. It is completely made of white marble. In front of the Taj Mahal is a long reflecting pool and gardens.

The white marble of the Taj Mahal shines in the moonlight. It looks like a scene from a fairy tale!

Which picture looks like the Taj Mahal?

THE TOWER OF PISA

The Tower of Pisa in Italy is the most famous tower in the world. And why? Not because it's so high or because it's so pretty—although it's a beautiful tower—but because it's leaning. It started leaning as soon as construction began. The ground was soft, so the tower began to sink on one side. But the builders kept on building. The higher it grew, the more it leaned!

The Tower of Pisa is seven floors high. It has been leaning since the builders started in 1137.

Which one looks the most like the real Tower of Pisa?

SAINT BASIL'S CATHEDRAL

Saint Basil's Cathedral is in the Red Square in Moscow, Russia. It looks like a fairy-tale castle with all of its beautiful colors and onion-shaped domes. The cathedral was built in 1555 and it has survived two big fires.

*Saint Basil's Cathedral
is a colorful sight on the Red Square.*

Can you find Saint Basil's Cathedral?

NEUSCHWANSTEIN CASTLE

Everyone loves a fairy tale. So King Ludwig II of Bavaria built himself a fairy-tale castle: Neuschwanstein. Here he could relax, high in the mountains and far away from his regular duties as a king. His castle has become famous because it was used as inspiration for the castle in the Disney movie *Sleeping Beauty*.

The fairy-tale castle Neuschwanstein was built high on a hill.

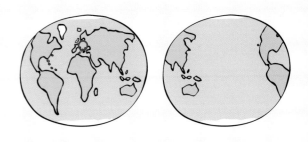

King Ludwig wanted his storybook castle to be only for himself. He requested that it be destroyed immediately after his death. Luckily, that did not happen. It is still standing tall and beautiful, high in the mountains.

THE BLUE MOSQUE

The Blue Mosque in Istanbul is actually gray, not blue.
But inside, many of the beautiful hand-painted tiles are blue.
The mosque is known not only for its colored tiles, but for its
great domes. In the center is a huge dome surrounded by many
small ones and six towers called minarets.

The Blue Mosque has six towers, or minarets.

The Blue Mosque looks like a collection of domes and towers. The domes are beautiful on the outside and the inside. They are made of thousands of colorful tiles.

THE ROYAL PALACE OF BANGKOK

The royal palace of Bangkok is also called the Grand Palace.
It is surrounded by a wall that is more than a mile long. Inside the wall
are about thirty palaces, temples, and other buildings. The buildings
are decorated with gemstones and other art treasures.

The marble temple of the Grand Palace.

Long ago, the palace was inhabited by the king, princesses, ministers, and thousands of servants. Today it is the official home of the Thai king, but he no longer lives there.

THE PALACE OF VERSAILLES

About three hundred years ago Louis XIV was the king of France. He was called the Sun King. He wanted the biggest and most beautiful palace in the world. Versailles has 700 rooms, more than 2,000 windows, 1,250 chimneys, and 67 staircases. Many of the walls were covered in gold and jewels.

The garden of Versailles is famous for its many ponds, beautiful fountains, and hundreds of statues.

Which of these things do you think didn't belong in Palace of Versailles?

LA SAGRADA FAMILIA

More than one hundred years ago, the construction of
the cathedral La Sagrada Familia started in Barcelona, Spain, and to this
day it is still not finished. The famous architect Gaudí designed
the building. Its towers look like dripstones, and it is surrounded
with interesting sculptures and decorations depicting saints and
exotic animals.

The front of La Sagrada Familia looks like an enormous cave with dripping stones and lots of statues hiding in it.

Building La Sagrada Familia is taking so long because it's incredibly complex. The windows are all handmade and the walls and towers are designed with hidden surprises like butterflies, dragonflies, and flowers.

THE BIG MOSQUE OF DJENNÉ

Djenné is located in Mali, Africa, on the edge of the desert. This special mosque is built from mud and clay, which are easy to find near the desert. When it rains the mud can get loose and the walls need to be repaired. Fortunately, it doesn't rain very often in Djenné.

The great mosque of Djenné is the largest mud building in the world.

Which building is the mosque of Djenné?

NOTRE-DAME CATHEDRAL

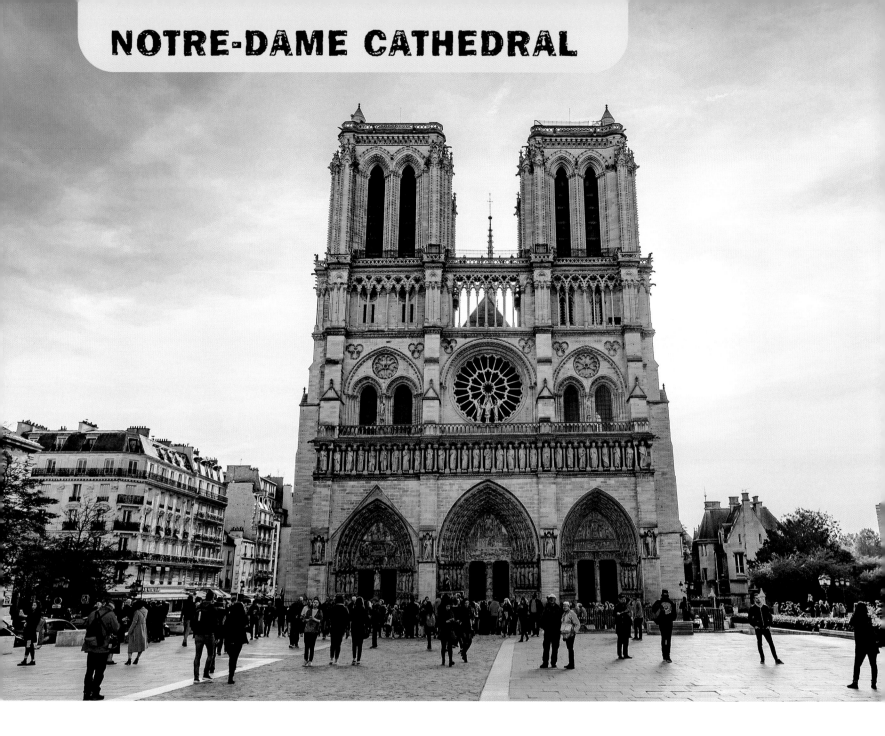

Notre-Dame is a very big cathedral in Paris. The building is bigger than an entire football field. It was built almost nine hundred years ago. In those days, churches were built as tall as possible, like a stairway to heaven. The cathedral looks even taller because of the thin, high windows.

Notre-Dame is on an island—
Isle de la Cité—in the center of Paris.

There are thousands of statues on the outside walls of Notre-Dame. Some of the statues look like monsters and are called gargoyles. The gargoyles help guide rain off the roof of the cathedral.

Big Ben in London is definitely the most famous clock tower in the world. The name Big Ben originally referred to the biggest iron bell inside the tower. It's beautiful sound rings out every hour. Smaller bells ring every fifteen minutes.

The tower is on the shore of the river Thames in London.
It is part of the House of Parliament, where the English laws are made.

Which tower looks like Big Ben?

THE UNITED STATES CAPITOL

The United States Capitol, D.C., is one of the most important buildings in the United States. It's the meeting place of Congress, which consists of representatives from each state. Congress makes the laws of the country. On top of the Capitol is a huge white dome, which looks a bit like the dome of the Pantheon in Rome. The dome makes the building look important.

Next to the Capitol is the White House.
It is the home of the president of
the United States of America.

Which building is the Capitol and which is the White House?

GALERIES LAFAYETTE

The first department stores were built over one hundred years ago. Galeries Lafayette in Paris is one of the most beautiful old department stores in the world. People come from all over to see the decorations, especially at Christmas.

Galeries Lafayette has ten floors.
On top of the roof you have a nice view
of Paris and the Eiffel Tower.

Galeries Lafayette looks more like
a museum than a store. The roof of
the store is just as beautiful as the inside.
The enormous dome is completely made
of stained glass.

THE SYDNEY OPERA HOUSE

Sydney is the largest city in Australia, with the biggest port.
As boats come into the harbor, passengers see the city with its many
tall buildings—and one building that looks very different. That is
the Sydney Opera House. A Danish architect designed the building
after being inspired by the ships in the harbor.

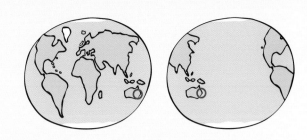

The roofs of the Sydney Opera House were designed to look like the sails of a ship.

Do you recognize the Sydney Opera House?

THE EMPIRE STATE BUILDING

The Empire State Building is the most famous building in New York. When it was first built in 1931, the skyscraper was the tallest in the world. It has more than a hundred floors—that is 1576 steps! How long would it take you to climb up all those stairs?

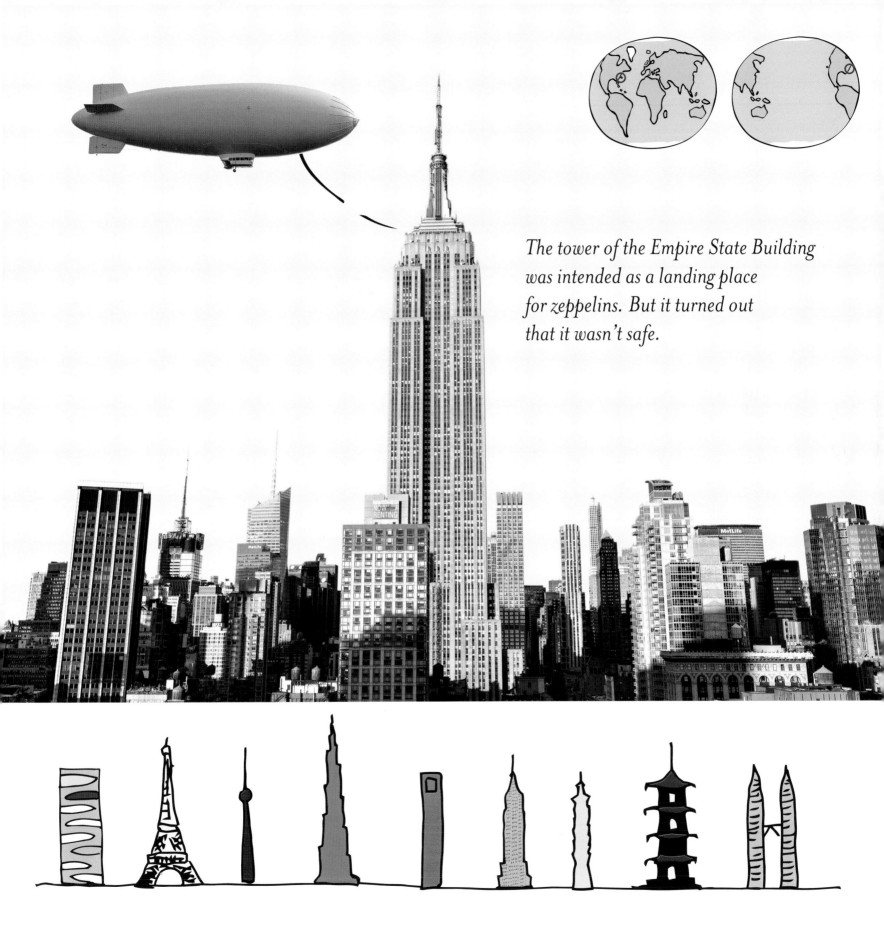

The tower of the Empire State Building was intended as a landing place for zeppelins. But it turned out that it wasn't safe.

Which building looks like the Empire State Building?

There's a very special building on a cliff above a Brazilian beach. It looks like a UFO, but it is the Niterói Contemporary Art Museum, or MAC. To get to the entrance you walk on a long red road that looks like a slide! The designer of the museum is the Brazilian architect Oscar Niemeyer.

The MAC, near Rio de Janeiro, looks like a spaceship!

The National Museum is also designed by Oscar Niemeyer. It's in Brasilia, the capital city of Brazil. What do you think of these two buildings? Do they look alike?

THE BURJ KHALIFA

The Burj Khalifa in Dubai, in the United Arab Emirates, is the tallest building in the world. You definitely will need an elevator to get to the top of the 163 floors! From its observation deck, it may seem like you can touch the clouds.

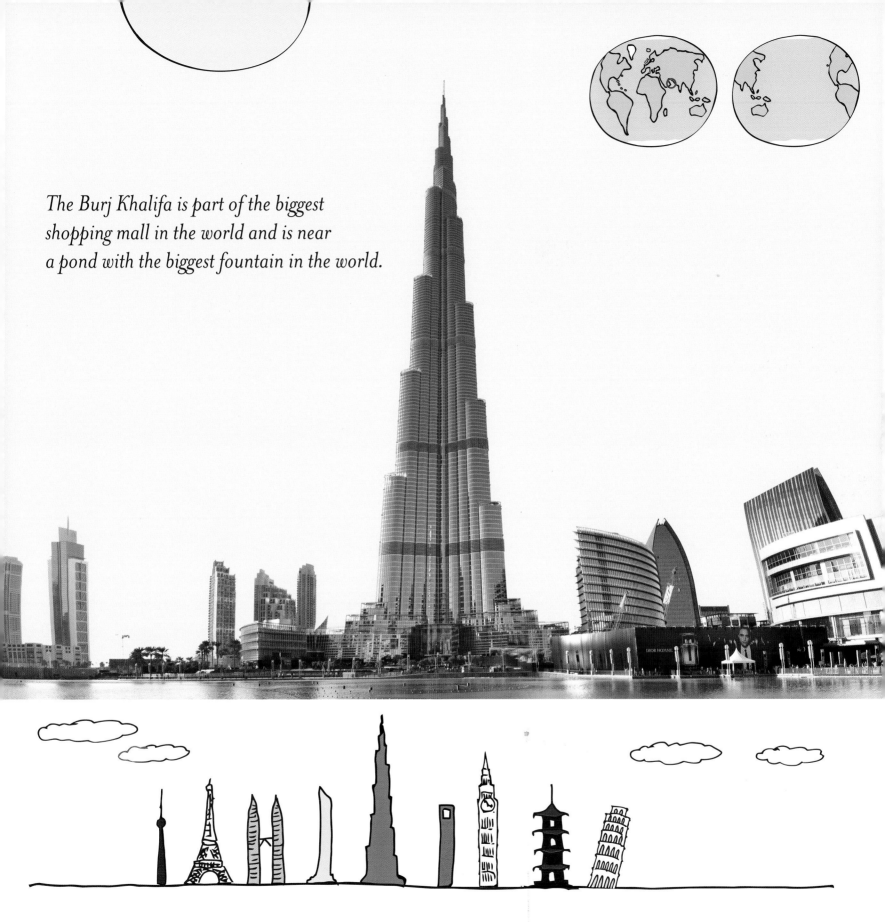

The Burj Khalifa is part of the biggest shopping mall in the world and is near a pond with the biggest fountain in the world.

Which tower looks like the Burj Khalifa?

Other famous structures

ANGKOR WAT

Hidden in the jungle of Cambodia is a temple called Angkor Wat. The name means "temple city," and it is the largest religious building in the world. The walls of Angkor Wat are completely swallowed by nature. Trees and vines grow straight through the rooftops. But that just adds to the beauty, don't you agree?

A tree grows straight through this wall on Angkor Wat.

Which building do you think is Angkor Wat?

THE PYRAMIDS

The pyramids of Egypt are one of the oldest monuments in the world. They were built from huge stones more than 4,500 years ago. Ancient Egyptians built the pyramids as monuments and burial places for the pharaohs and their families. It took thousands of workers many years to build the pyramids. The Great Pyramid took twenty-three years to build.

A stone sphinx guards the pyramid. A sphinx has the head of a human and the body of a lion.

Pharaohs were buried in secret rooms. Their bodies were wrapped in cloths and placed in beautifully decorated tombs along with many valuables. The ancient Egyptians believed that their pharaoh would need his riches in the afterlife.

THE GREAT WALL OF CHINA

The Great Wall of China winds for more than 5,500 miles across China! It is truly one of the great wonders of the world. The wall was built more than a thousand years ago to protect the country against enemies. Soldiers could stand in the towers to keep watch and protect their country. If an enemy was approaching, soldiers built fires and sent smoke signals to warn fellow soldiers at nearby towers.

The Great Wall of China twists over the mountains like a sleeping dragon.

How many watchtowers do you count on this part of the Great Wall?

MACHU PICCHU

Another wonder of the world is Machu Picchu, also known as the lost city of the Incas. Machu Picchu is an ancient city high in the mountains of Peru in South America. The city is so high that it was discovered centuries after the Incas were gone. Researchers believe that Machu Picchu once was a very wealthy city, and today it is still very beautiful.

Now there are no longer Incas
living in Machu Picchu.
But there are llamas.

Which animals might you find in Machu Picchu?

THE EIFFEL TOWER

The Eiffel Tower was built as part of the World's Fair in Paris, France, in 1889. It was named after Gustave Eiffel, the engineer whose company built it. People thought it would only stand strong for twenty years, but the Eiffel Tower is still there today. Tourists from all over the world visit and take photos of it, because you've only been in Paris if you see the Eiffel Tower!

Sometimes the Eiffel Tower is lit up in the colors of the French flag for celebrations.

Which Eiffel Tower is celebrating?

THE GOLDEN GATE BRIDGE

The Golden Gate Bridge is a beautiful bridge near San Francisco, California. It is one of the longest suspension bridges in the world. Every day, thousands of cars drive across the bridge to and from San Francisco. The bridge may be called golden, but it is actually red.

*The Golden Gate Bridge is named after
a time when people from all over the world
came to this area in search of gold.*

Can you point to the Golden Gate Bridge?

The Statue of Liberty was a gift from France to the United States to celebrate a hundred years of freedom. The statue was made in Paris and shipped to the United States in parts. Now she is standing in the harbor of New York with a burning torch in her hand to welcome tourists and new Americans.

You can walk into the crown of the Statue of Liberty and enjoy a stunning view.

Which statue looks most like the Statue of Liberty?

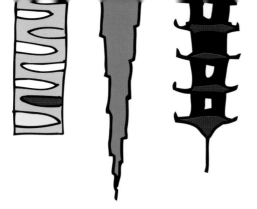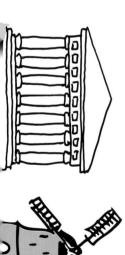